CW00971738

Twenty-One Poems

Twenty-One Poems

Atal Bihari Vajpayee

Translated by
Pavan K. Varma

VIKING

VIKING

Penguin Books India (P) Ltd., 11 Community Centre, Panchsheel
Park, New Delhi 110017, India
Penguin Books Ltd., 80 Strand, London WC2R 0RL, UK
Penguin Putnam Inc., 375 Hudson Street, New York, New York
10014, USA
Penguin Books Australia Ltd., 250 Camberwell Road, Camberwell,
Victoria 3124, Australia
Penguin Books Canada Ltd., 10 Alcorn Avenue, Suite 300,
Toronto, Ontario M4V 3B2, Canada
Penguin Books (NZ) Ltd., Cnr Rosedale & Airborne Roads,
Albany, Auckland, New Zealand

First published in Viking by Penguin Books India 2001

Copyright © Atal Bihari Vajpayee 2001

This translation copyright © Pavan K. Varma 2001

All rights reserved

10 9 8 7 6 5 4 3 2 1

Typeset in Walkman-Hindi and Sabon by S.R. Enterprises, New
Delhi

Printed at Saurabh Print-O-Pack, Noida

This book is sold subject to the condition that it shall not, by way of
trade or otherwise, be lent, resold, hired out, or otherwise circulated
without the publisher's prior written consent in any form of binding
or cover other than that in which it is published and without a
similar condition including this condition being imposed on the
subsequent purchaser and without limiting the rights under copyright
reserved above, no part of this publication may be reproduced,
stored in or introduced into a retrieval system, or transmitted in any
form or by any means (electronic, mechanical, photocopying,
recording or otherwise), without the prior written permission of
both the copyright owner and the above-mentioned publisher of
this book.

नेहा के नाम
For Neha

क्रमांक

Contents

Author's Note

It sometimes surprises me that people should want to publish my poetry. I am not a man of letters, nor do I claim to be an intellectual. I write to make sense of my world, and for strength to face the challenges of life. My concerns are those of any man alive to his own life and to the life of those around him. My poetry is, to me, not an expression of regret or defeat but of confidence, and a will to win.

Poetry came to me as an inheritance. My father, Pandit Krishna Bihari Vajpayee, was a well-known and respected poet of the historic city of Gwalior. I still remember many of his works, including his most popular one, *'Eeshwar Prarthana'* (Prayer to the Almighty), which was sung at school assemblies in Gwalior. My grandfather, Pandit Shyamlal Vajpayee, though not a poet himself, had an abiding love for both Hindi and Sanskrit literature.

Given this literary atmosphere at home, it is not surprising that my elder brother, Pandit Avadh

Bihari Vajpayee, also took to writing poetry, and soon I was doing so too. I began frequenting *kavi sammelans*, or poetry gatherings, first as part of the audience and then as a 'promising' young poet. Of my early attempts I remember only one. It was about the Taj Mahal, not about its beauty, but the exploitation and suffering that marked its construction.

Some friends say that had I not been a politician, I would have been a leading Hindi poet. I don't know about that, but there is no doubt in my mind that politics did interfere with my evolution as a poet. Yet it wasn't politics alone. When I abandoned my studies in law to take over as editor of the monthly magazine *Rashtradharma*, published from Lucknow, I had little time to devote to my poetry, and even less after I started editing weeklies and dailies. Creative writing, especially the writing of verse, demands not just time but also a conducive environment. Flights of the imagination are almost impossible if you have to worry constantly about tight deadlines. It was simpler, then, to express my thoughts in short articles.

After I joined politics, even the writing of simple prose became difficult. Whatever energy I had was taken up by speeches. In 1957, I became a member of the Lok Sabha, the Lower House of Parliament, for the first time, and speeches became my primary means of expression. Rarely could I find the time for poetry. After assuming the responsibilities of the government in 1998, I find even less time to write, or even read, poetry.

It has been my experience that poetry and politics rarely go together. In poetry one communicates, primarily, with oneself. In politics, there is always the subtle danger of ignoring the self in the process of communicating regularly with some mass gathering or the other. Poetry brooks no compromise with the freedom and the integrity of the creative voice. Politics, on the other hand, often bows to the compulsion of circumstances and the common denominator of consensus. Of course, the latter is not to be derided or belittled for that reason. Politics has its own honoured place in a nation's life, and I have no regrets that it became the main calling in my life.

What I do regret is that I haven't written as much poetry as I would have liked to. But I have tried, always, to be true to the poet inside me, who cannot ignore the realities of his time. I have paid a price for this; yet I continue with my aim to combine my concerns as a writer with my concerns as a political worker. Sometimes I am overcome by an urge to leave it all behind and lose myself in books, writing, and thought. But I have been unable to do that. I have lived over seven decades caught in this dilemma, and what is left of my life will probably be spent no differently.

A few words about my thoughts on English. The ship of history brought English to India's shores. It was the language of our colonial masters. We sent the colonial rulers back more than five decades ago, but just as she has accepted so much else that is life-nourishing from the rest of the world, India retained English, assimilated it, and made it her own. It is a rich language and has benefited us immensely. We are proud that many Indians have further enriched it with their creativity and intellectual brilliance. English can hardly be called an alien language today. It has joined the sisterhood of Indian languages, which constitute such a cherished part of our diversity.

And like other Indian languages, English too has been making its own distincitve contribution to the dynamic unity that underlies India's diversity.

At the same time, I do believe that the Indianization of English is still an incomplete affair. English may have become the natural language for commerce and business, and also for governmental functioning at higher levels, but it is spoken only by a small minority of Indians, many of whom continue to be rooted in their mother tongues. It still does not adequately capture, especially in literature, the multi-layered and richly-nuanced cultural, social and emotional life of one billion Indians. An authentic portrayal of India in literature still seems to take place best in non-English Indian languages. And translation of good Indian literature into English and other international languages has not yet happened to the desired extent.

I am grateful to all those who have worked to take my poems to an international audience through this collection. I hope that these poems, both the originals and the translated versions, will please the reader. Hindi poetry has its own conventions and imagery that are often lost in translation. The twenty-one poems chosen for this collection are those that I felt would translate best into English, and also constitute a representative sample of my attempts at verse over the years. What was important to me was that the translations communicate the sensibility and the mood of the Hindi originals, and Pavan Varma's English renderings succeed in doing that.

Translator's Note

To translate the work of Atal Bihari Vajpayee, the poet (who is also the Prime Minister of India) was a joy and a revelation. The Prime Minister of India is not the author of this collection of poems. The author is, for the greatest part, A.B. Vajpayee, the individual. Not surprisingly, the poems cover the entire gamut of emotions that a human being is heir to: hope, despair, joy, doubt, anger, sorrow, love and resolve. There is something deeply personal in many of the poems, providing an insight into the private world of a figure who has lived so much of his life in the public realm.

As one of India's most well known political personalities, Mr Vajpayee's public life is familiar to the people of India. But behind the outer facade there is a private person who, while deeply involved in politics, is more than merely the sum total of his political beliefs and achievements. When in jail he laments the fact that the sky has been shut out. On his birthday he thinks aloud about the ultimate value of one more year being added to an essentially finite life. He is honest enough to admit to doubt about the final worth of his existence. He is human enough to sometimes wonder whether the sacrifice is worth the effort, or the effort worth the sacrifice. He is realistic enough to occasionally question the promise of idealism, but not cynical enough to question its relevance. Above all, he is willing to live with imperfections in his own life because life itself is not entirely rational or free of blemish.

These are the themes of Mr Vajpayee's poetry. His verse is disarmingly simple. There is no attempt at linguistic or intellectual complexity merely to impress, and this ensures a rare sincerity and immediacy. The poems echo the voice of the heart, put down without ceremony.

I believe that the twenty-one poems included in this selection are representative of Mr Vajpayee's larger body of work. We have excluded most of the declamatory and hortatory poems, which are more appropriate for a political stage. Most of the poems here are about Mr Vajpayee, the man, although there are some which also point to Mr Vajpayee, the political person. The truth, of course, is that honest poetry cannot be written unless a person is true both to his public and private selves.

Translation is not easy. It is often a thankless job. Poetry in translation can very rarely capture the magic of the original. Someone has said that translating poetry is like transferring perfume from one bottle to another: some of the fragrance is bound to be lost. The perennial problem before a translator is to accomplish his task without allowing the translation to become a soulless paraphrasing. Even as he captures the meaning and intent of the original, a translator must, I believe, seek to do so, to the greatest extent possible, by making the translation readable within the framework of poetry.

In many ways Mr Vajpayee belongs to the old, classical school of Hindi poetry. Rhyme and metre are important to him, and he employs images and symbols peculiar to traditional Hindi literature. Much of this is virtually impossible to capture in modern English. My attempt has been to make the translations work as poems in themselves, while retaining the meaning, mood and the essential music of the originals. To achieve this, in a few places I have taken the liberty to 'transcreate'.

These are among the first translations of Mr Vajpayee's poetry into English, and hopefully this will lead to a much wider pan-Indian and global audience for his writings. I have greatly enjoyed translating the poems, especially for the insight they provide into the inner world of the Prime Minister of India. I will always cherish the occasional meetings I had with him during the preparation of this work.

I am grateful to Rohit Babbar, Ghansham Dass and Rominder Singh, who, in Delhi and in Cyprus, helped so willingly in the typing and preparation of the manuscript. Ravi Singh in Penguin was a very valuable mentor. David Davidar was, as always, the insightful editor, friend and guide. Ajay Bisaria, in the Prime Minister's Office, was involved from the very beginning in the project and proved to be a pillar of support.

I owe a debt of gratitude to my mother, Shakuntala Varma, now seventy-eight, who, in spite of her fragile health, read the manuscript and offered very perceptive advice. I regard her as a truly composite Indian. She speaks the Queen's English, but even better Hindi; she can recite the *Ramayana* almost entirely from memory, and is fluent in Bhojpuri. Finally, for my wife, Renuka, I have, as with my other books, only this to say: thank you very much.

Twenty-One Poems
इक्कीस कविताऐं

नए मील का पत्थर

नए मील का पत्थर पार हुआ।

कितने पत्थर शेष न कोई जानता!
    अन्तिम कौन पड़ाव नहीं पहचानता।
अक्षय सूरज, अखण्ड धरती,
    केवल काया, जीती-मरती,
इसलिए उम्र का बढ़ना भी त्यौहार हुआ।
    नए मील का पत्थर पार हुआ।

बचपन याद बहुत आता है,
    यौवन रसघट भर लाता है,
बदला मौसम, ढलती छाया,
    रिसती गागर, लुटती माया,
सब कुछ दाँव लगाकर घाटे का व्यापार हुआ।
    नए मील का पत्थर पार हुआ।

A New Milestone

And so a new milestone's been crossed.

How many more remain, no one knows,
        And no one knows when the final
            destination will arrive.
The sun is imperishable, the earth indestructible,
        Only the body lives and dies;
Another year added is cause for celebration.
        A new milestone's been crossed.

Memories of childhood have overwhelmed me at
    times,
        At times the exhilaration of youth has
            flooded my mind,
But the season's turned, the shadows lengthen,
        The vessel's drained, all enchantments fade,
Though I staked all I had, it's been a contract of
    loss.
        A new milestone's been crossed.

वेदना

कोठरी सूनी
वेदना दूनी

    झींगुरों का स्वर
    वेधता अन्तर

बंद है आकाश
घुट रहा निःश्वास।

Anguish

This desolate cell
The heart's anguish swells

    The chirping of crickets
    Slices through me

The sky shut out
I cannot breathe.

एक बरस बीत गया

एक बरस बीत गया
    झुलसाता जेठ मास
    शरद चाँदनी उदास
    सिसकी भरते सावन का
    अन्तर्घट रीत गया
    एक बरस बीत गया।
सीकचों में सिमटा जग
किन्तु विकल प्राण विहग
धरती से अम्बर तक
गूँज मुक्ति गीत गया,
    एक बरस बीत गया।
    पथ निहारत नयन
    गिनते दिन, पल, छिन
    लौट कभी आएगा
    मन का जो मीत गया,
एक बरस बीत गया।

A Year Has Gone By

A year has gone by.
    The burning month of May
    The desolate moon of autumn
    The sobbing monsoon too has spent itself
    And its heart is dry.
    A year has gone by.

The world cowers behind bars
But the unquiet soul takes wing,
From the earth to the sky
Echoes the song of freedom.
    A year has gone by.

My eyes scan the pathway
Counting days, hours, moments:
Perhaps my muse, who has gone away
Will return one day.
    A year has gone by.

दो चतुष्पदी

वही मंज़िल
वही कमरा
वही खिड़की
वही पहरा

राज बदला
ताज बदला
पर नहीं
समाज बदला।

Two Quatrains

The same goal
The same room
    The same window
    The same guard, unchanged

The kingdom's changed
The crown's changed
    But the social order
    Remains unchanged.

नई गाँठ लगती

जीवन की डोर छोर छूने को मचली,
जाड़े की धूप स्वर्ण कलशों से फिसली,
          अन्तर की अमराई
          सोई पड़ी शहनाई,
एक दबे दर्द-सी सहसा ही जगती।
          नई गाँठ लगती।

दूर नहीं, पास नहीं, मंज़िल अजानी,
साँसों के सरगम पर चलने की ठानी,
          पानी पर लकीर-सी,
          खुली जंजीर-सी।
कोई मृगतृष्णा मुझे बार-बार छलती।
          नई गाँठ लगती।

मन में लगी जो गाँठ मुश्किल से खुलती,
दागदार ज़िन्दगी न घाटों पर धुलती,
          जैसी की तैसी नहीं,
          जैसी है वैसी सही,
कबिरा की चादरिया बड़े भाग मिलती।
          नई गाँठ लगती।

A New Knot Is Tied

The river of life seeks the Ocean again,
The winter sun slips down like golden rain,
    In the heart, the mango grove's fragrance,
    The *shehnai's* lost cadence
Like a pain, half-forgotten, comes suddenly alive.
    A new knot is tied.

Not far, not near, the goal is unknown,
Yet to life's rhythm, I resolve to move on:
    A pattern drawn on water,
    All shackles undone—
Again, and again, by a mirage I am enticed.
    A new knot is tied.

A knot tied in the mind, is not easily unravelled,
A life, deeply marked, is not easily cleansed,
    Not to give as one gets,
    But to accept what one gets,
Only the very fortunate have Kabir's cloth of life.*
    A new knot is tied.

---

* The expression 'chadariya' is symbolic of the freedom we all have
to weave the fabric of our lives.

ऊँचाई

ऊँचे पहाड़ पर,
पेड़ नहीं लगते,
पौधे नहीं उगते,
न घास ही जमती है।

जमती है सिर्फ बर्फ,
जो कफन की तरह सफेद और
मौत की तरह ठंडी होती है।
खेलती, खिलखिलाती नदी,
जिसका रूप धारण कर
अपने भाग्य पर बूँद-बूँद रोती है।

ऐसी ऊँचाई,
जिसका परस,
पानी को पत्थर कर दे,
ऐसी ऊँचाई
जिसका दरस हीन भाव भर दे,
अभिनन्दन की अधिकारी है,
उस पर झण्डे गाड़े जा सकते हैं,

Never Place Me So High

On a very high mountain
Trees cannot take root,
Plants do not grow,
Grass will not survive.

> Only snow remains,
> White as the shroud
> And cold as death.
> Here, each drop that will make
> The gurgling, playful river,
> Mourns its fate.

A height
Whose touch alone
Turns water to stone,
Such height,
That merely to look upon it is to feel small,
May be deserving of praise,
An invitation to tireless climbers,
A good place to plant your flag.

किंतु कोई गौरैया,
वहाँ नीड़ नहीं बना सकती,
न कोई थका-माँदा बटोही,
उसकी छाँव में पलभर पलक ही झपका सकता है।

सच्चाई यह है कि
केवल ऊँचाई ही काफी नहीं होती,
सबसे अलग-थलग
परिवेश से पृथक,
अपनों से कटा-बँटा,
शून्य में अकेला खड़ा होना,
पहाड़ की महानता नहीं,
मजबूरी है।
ऊँचाई और गहराई में
आकाश-पाताल की दूरी है।

जो जितना ऊँचा,
उतना ही एकाकी होता है,
हर भार को स्वयं ही ढोता है,
चेहरे पर मुस्कानें चिपका,
मन ही मन रोता है।

But no sparrow
Can build a nest there,
Nor a tired traveller rest
Even for a moment in its shadow.

This, then, is the truth:
Mere height is never enough;
To stand apart
Without a context,
Severed from one's own,
A lone hermit in a void,
Is not the mountain's greatness,
Only its compulsion:
Height and depth
Are as separate and distant
As heaven and earth.

A person is as solitary
As the height to which he rises,
He bears his burdens alone,
Wears his smiles, and weeps unseen.

जरूरी यह है कि
    ऊँचाई के साथ विस्तार भी हो,
    जिससे मनुष्य
    ठूँठ-सा खड़ा न रहे,
    औरों से घुले-मिले,
    किसी को साथ ले,
    किसी के संग चले।

भीड़ में खो जाना,
यादों में डूब जाना,
स्वंय को भूल जाना,

    अस्तित्व को अर्थ,
    जीवन को सुगन्ध देता है।

धरती को बौनों की नहीं,
ऊँचे कद के इंसानों की जरूरत है।
इतने ऊँचे कि आसमान को छू लें,
नये नक्षत्रों में प्रतिभा के बीज बो लें,
    किंतु इतने ऊँचे भी नहीं,
    कि पाँव तले दूब ही न जमे,
    कोई काँटा न चुभे,
    कोई कली न खिले।

What matters is this:
>That there be expanse with height,
>So that a man
>Is not fixed and dead as a stump,
>But blends in and belongs with others,
>Winning some to his cause,
>Falling in step with others.

To be lost in the crowd,
To be immersed in remembrance,
To forget oneself,

>Gives fragrance to life,
>A meaning to existence.

Not dwarfs, the earth needs men
Who will stand tall.
So tall, they touch the sky
And seed new galaxies with brilliance,
>Yet, not so tall
>That tender grass does not grow,
>No thorns tear the skin,
>No flowers bloom.

न वसंत हो, न पतझड़,
हो सिर्फ ऊँचाई का अंधड़,
मात्र अकेलेपन का सन्नाटा।

मेरे प्रभु!
मुझे इतनी ऊँचाई कभी मत देना
गैरों को गले न लगा सकूँ
इतनी रुखाई कभी मत देना।

No spring, no autumn,
Only the storms of great heights
And the numbing stillness of solitude—

My lord!
Never place me so high,
That I cannot embrace
Those who are not my own.

रोते–रोते रात सो गई

झुकी न अलकें
झपी न पलकें
सुधियों की बारात खो गई।

दर्द पुराना,
मीत न जाना,
बातों में ही प्राप्त हो गई।

घुमड़ी बदली,
बूँद न निकली,
बिछुड़न ऐसी व्यथा बो गई।

Night's Passage

No cascading hair,
No luminous eyes,
The procession of memories has lost its bearings.

An ancient pain,
The beloved unknowing,
Though we talked through the night and into
morning.

Darkening clouds,
Not a drop of rain,
Separation has sown such seeds of suffering.

कौरव कौन, कौन पाण्डव

कौरव कौन
कौन पाण्डव,
टेढ़ा सवाल है।
दोनों और शकुनि
का फैला
कूट जाल है।
धर्मराज ने छोड़ी नहीं
जुए की लत है।
हर पंचायत में
पांचाली
अपमानित है।
बिना कृष्ण के
आज
महाभारत होना है,
कोई राजा बने,
रंक को तो रोना है।

Who Are the Kauravas, and Who the Pandavas

Who are the Kauravas
And who the Pandavas,
Is a difficult question to ask.
Shakuni's evil net,
Cast wide,
Caught them both in its grasp.
Dharmaraj has not overcome
His addiction to dice.
In every panchayat
Draupadi is robbed of her honour.
Without Krishna
Today
The *Mahabharata* will be fought,
No matter who claims the throne,
The poor will continue to suffer.

मन का संतोष

पृथिवी पर
मनुष्य ही ऐसा एक प्राणी है,
जो भीड़ में अकेला, और,
अकेले में भीड़ से घिरा अनुभव करता है।

मनुष्य को झुण्ड में रहना पसंद है।
घर-परिवार से प्रारम्भ कर,
वह बस्तियाँ बसाता है।
गली-ग्राम-पुर-नगर सजाता है।

सभ्यता की निष्ठुर दौड़ में,
संस्कृति को पीछे छोड़ता हुआ,
प्रकृति पर विजय,
मृत्यु को मुट्ठी में करना चाहता है।

अपनी रक्षा के लिए
औरों के विनाश के सामान जुटाता है।
आकाश को अभिशप्त,
धरती को निर्वसन,
वायु को विषाक्त,
जल को दूषित करने में संकोच नहीं करता।

Peace of Mind

On earth, among the living,
Only a human being
Feels alone in a crowd, and
Besieged by crowds when alone.

      Man prefers the company of his kind.
      He starts a family, builds a home,
      Puts up whole settlements.
      Adorns a street, a village, a town, a city.

In the cruel march of civilization,
He casts culture aside,
Seeks victory over nature,
Demands the surrender of death.

      To protect himself and only his own,
      He gathers means to destroy all others.
      Nothing will faze him:
      Damn the sky,
      Strip the earth,
      Pollute the waters,
      Poison the air.

किंतु, यह सब कुछ करने के बाद
जब वह एकांत में बैठकर विचार करता है,
वह एकान्त, फिर घर का कोना हो,
या कोलाहल से भरा बाजार,
या प्रकाश की गति से तेज उड़ता जहाज,
या कोई वैज्ञानिक प्रयोगशाला,
या मंदिर
या मरघट।

जब वह आत्मालोचन करता है,
मन की परतें खोलता है,
स्वयं से बोलता है,
हानि-लाभ का लेखा-जोखा नहीं,
क्या खोया, क्या पाया का हिसाब भी नहीं,
जब वह पूरी जिन्दगी को ही तौलता है,
निर्ममता से निरखता, परखता है,
तब वह अपने मन से क्या कहता है!
इसी का महत्त्व है, यही उसका सत्य है।

अंतिम यात्रा के अवसर पर,
विदा की वेला में,
जब सबका साथ छूटने लगता है,
शरीर भी साथ नहीं देता,
तब आत्मग्लानि से मुक्त

But when all this is done,
When he finally sits down to think, all by himself,
In a quiet corner of his home,
Or in the cacophony of the bazaar,
In a plane travelling faster than light,
In some laboratory of science,
In a temple
Or a crematorium—

When he introspects,
Peels away the many layers of his mind,
Speaks to himself,
Not about profit and loss,
Or even about what was won or lost,
When he puts all his life in the balance,
Judges himself by his own touchstone,
Adds it all up, without mercy—
What, then, does he say to himself!
That alone has worth, that alone is his truth.

On the occasion of that final journey,
At the moment of parting,
When all bonds begin to give way,
When the body too is no longer one's own,
Then, free of self-reproach,

यदि कोई हाथ उठाकर यह कह सकता है
कि उसने जीवन में जो कुछ किया,
सही समझकर किया,
किसी को जानबूझकर चोट पहुँचाने के लिए नहीं,
सहज कर्म समझकर किया,
तो उसका अस्तित्व सार्थक है,
उसका जीवन सफल है।

उसी के लिए यह कहावत बनी है,
मन चंगा तो कठौती में गंगाजल है।

If a man can raise his hand and say
That whatever he did in life,
He did because it was right,
He did it not to cause pain,
But as his selfless karma,
Then his existence has meaning,
His life has been successful.

Indeed, the proverb was made for such a
one:
'If the mind be pure, the Ganga will be found
even in a bowl.'

अपने ही मन से कुछ बोलें

क्या खोया, क्या पाया जग में,
मिलते और बिछड़ते मग में,
मुझे किसी से नहीं शिकायत,
यद्यपि छला गया पग-पग में,
एक दृष्टि बीती पर डालें, यादों की पोटली टटोलें।

पृथिवी लाखों वर्ष पुरानी,
जीवन एक अनन्त कहानी,
पर तन की अपनी सीमाएँ,
यद्यपि सौ शरदों की वाणी,
इतना काफी है अंतिम दस्तक पर खुद दरवाजा खोलें।

जन्म-मरण का अविरत फेरा,
जीवन बंजारों का डेरा,
आज यहाँ, कल कहाँ कूच है,
कौन जानता, किधर सवेरा,
अँधियारा आकाश असीमित, प्राणों के पंखो को तौलें।
अपने ही मन से कुछ बोलें!

Let Us Speak to Our Own Selves

What have I lost or gained on earth?
In this journey of meeting and separation
I've known deception at every step,
But I have no grievance, no complaints,
As I appraise the past, sift through memories.

The earth is a million years old,
And life a story without an end,
But the body has its limitations
Though it longs to last a hundred autumns.
I will be content if at that last knock, I open the
    door on my own.

The ceaseless wheel of birth and death,
This life, like a gypsies' camp,
Here today, a new journey tomorrow,
Who knows where dawn will break—
The dark sky stretches on for ever, let us test the
    wings of life.

Let us speak to our own selves.

राह कौन-सी जाऊँ मैं?

चौराहे पर लुटता चीर,
प्यादे से पिट गया वजीर,
चलूँ आखिरी चाल कि बाजी छोड़ विरक्ति रचाऊँ मैं?
राह कौन-सी जाऊँ मैं?

सपना जन्मा और मर गया,
मधु ऋतु में ही बाग झर गया,
तिनके बिखरे हुए बटोरूँ या नव सृष्टि सजाऊँ मैं?
राह कौन-सी जाऊँ मैं?

दो दिन मिले उधार में,
घाटे के व्यापार में,
क्षण-क्षण का हिसाब जोड़ूँ या पूँजी शेष लुटाऊँ मैं?
राह कौन-सी जाऊँ मैं?

What Road Should I Go Down?

Honour lost at busy crossroads,
Knights defeated by pawns:
Do I make my final move, or do I withdraw from
battle?
What road should I go down?

A dream was born, and died,
The garden dried up in the season of spring:
Do I gather these scattered leaves, or do I fashion
a new universe?
What road should I go down?

Two days, on loan, is all I've earned
In a bargain already lost:
Do I take stock of each moment, or do I squander
what little remains?
What road should I go down?

सत्ता

मासूम बच्चों,
बूढ़ी औरतों,
जवान मर्दों,
की लाशों के ढेर पर चढ़ कर
जो सत्ता के सिंहासन तक पहुँचना चाहते हैं
उनसे मेरा एक सवाल है:
        क्या मरने वालों के साथ
        उनका कोई रिश्ता न था?
न सही धर्म का नाता,
क्या धरती का भी संबंध नहीं था?
'पृथिवी माँ और हम उसके पुत्र हैं।'
अथर्ववेद का यह मंत्र
क्या सिर्फ जपने के लिए है,
जीने के लिए नहीं?

        आग में जले बच्चे,
        वासना की शिकार औरतें,
        राख में बदले घर
        न सभ्यता का प्रमाण पत्र हैं,
        न देश-भक्ति का तमगा,

Power

To those who try to reach
The throne of power
Over mounds of dead bodies
Of innocent children
Old women
Young men,
I have a question:
>Did nothing bind them
>To those who died?
Their faiths differed;
Was it not enough that they too were of this earth?
'The earth is our mother, and we are her sons':
This mantra from the Atharvaveda,
Is it only to be chanted, not lived?

>Children charred by fire,
>Women savaged by lust,
>Houses reduced to ash
>Constitute neither a certificate of culture
>Nor a badge of patriotism,

वे यदि घोषणा-पत्र हैं तो पशुता का,
प्रमाण हैं तो पतितावस्था का,
ऐसे कपूतों से
माँ का निपूती रहना ही अच्छा था,
        निर्दोष रक्त से सनी राजगद्दी,
        श्मशान की धूल से भी गिरी है,
        सत्ता की अनियंत्रित भूख
        रक्त-पिपासा से भी बुरी है।

They are proof of bestiality,
Proof of degradation,
And if these be the deeds of sons,
Mothers should not wish for any.
>A throne smeared with the blood of the
>>innocent
>Ranks lower than the dust of a cemetery,
>The lust for absolute power is worse
>Than a thirst for blood.

मौत से ठन गई

ठन गई!
मौत से ठन गई!

जूझने का मेरा कोई इरादा न था,
मोड़ पर मिलेंगे इसका वादा न था,
रास्ता रोक कर वह खड़ी हो गई,
यों लगा जिन्दगी से बड़ी हो गई।

मौत की उम्र क्या? दो पल भी नहीं,
जिन्दगी-सिलसिला, आज कल की नहीं,
मैं जी भर जिया, मैं मन से मरूँ,
लौटकर आऊँगा, कूच से क्या डरूँ?

तू दबे पाँव, चोरी-छिपे से न आ,
सामने वार कर, फिर मुझे आजमा।
मौत से बेखबर, जिन्दगी का सफर,
शाम हर सुरमई, रात बंसी का स्वर,
बात ऐसी नहीं कि कोई गम ही नहीं,
दर्द अपने-पराए कुछ कम भी नहीं।

A Battle with Death

A battle with death!
What a battle it will be!

I had no plans to take her on,
We had not agreed to meet at that curve,
Yet there she stood, blocking my path,
Looming larger than life.

How long does death last? A moment, perhaps
two—
Life is a sequence, beyond today and tomorrow.
I have lived to the full, I will die as I choose,
I will return, I have no fear of letting go.

So do not come by stealth, and take me by surprise,
Come, test me: meet me head on.
Unheeding of death, life's journey unfolds,
Evenings sketched with kohl, nights
smooth as the flute's notes,
I do not say there was no pain,
There were sorrows, of my own and of this world.

प्यार इतना परायों से मुझको मिला,
न अपनों से बाकी है कोई गिला,
हर चुनौती से दो हाथ मैंने किए,
आँधियों में जलाए हैं बुझते दिए,
आज झकझोरता तेज तूफान है,
नाव भँवरों की बाँहों में मेहमान है,

पार पाने का कायम मगर हौसला,
देख तूफां का तेवर तरी तन गई,
मौत से ठन गई।

And such love I received from those not
        mine,
No grievance remains against those who
        were mine,
I grappled with every challenge thrown my way,
Lit brave little lamps in violent squalls.
        A savage storm rages today,
        The boat is a brief guest in the whirlpool's
        embrace,

Yet the resolve to sail across is firm,
The storm flashes its fury, this boat will take it on,
        With death, what a battle it will be!

न दैन्यं न पलायनम्

कर्तव्य के पुनीत पथ को
हमने खेद से सींचा है,
कभी-कभी अपने अश्रु और-
प्राणों का अर्घ्य भी दिया है।

किन्तु, अपनी ध्येय-मात्रा में—
हम कभी रूके नहीं हैं।
किसी चुनौती के सम्मुख
कभी झुके नहीं है।

आज,
जब कि राष्ट्र-जीवन की
समस्त निधियाँ,
दाँव पर लगी हैं,
और,
एक घनीभूत अँधेरा—
हमारे जीवन के
सारे आलोक को
निगल लेना चाहता है;

Resolve

The pure path of duty
We have drenched with our sweat,
Sometimes we have given it our tears,
At times made an offering of our life.

> But in the journey to our goal
> We have never faltered.
> Whatever be the challenge
> We have never been daunted.

Today,
When all our values
Are at stake,
And
A dense darkness
Threatens to devour
All the light
Of our lives,

हमें ध्येय के लिए
जीने, जूझने और
आवश्यकता पड़ने पर—
मरने के संकल्प को दोहराना है।

आग्नेय परीक्षा की
इस घड़ी में—
आइए, अर्जुन की तरह
उद्घोष करें:
'न दैन्यं न पलायनम्।'

We must reiterate
Our resolve to live,
To fight for, and if necessary,
To die for the goal.

In this moment
Of ordeal by fire,
Let us, like Arjuna proclaim:
We will not cower, nor shall we quit.

झुक नहीं सकते

टूट सकते हैं मगर हम झुक नहीं सकते।
सत्य का संघर्ष सत्ता से,
न्याय लड़ता निरंकुशता से,
अँधेरे ने दी चुनौती है,
किरण अन्तिम अस्त होती है।

दीप निष्ठा का लिए निष्कम्प,
वज्र टूटे या उठे भूकम्प,
यह बराबर का नहीं है युद्ध,
हम निहत्थे, शत्रु है सन्नद्ध,
हर तरह के शस्त्र से है सज्ज,
और पशुबल हो उठा निर्लज्ज।

किन्तु फिर भी जूझने का प्रण,
पुनः अंगद ने बढ़ाया चरण
प्राण-पण से करेंगे प्रतिकार,
समर्पण की माँग अस्वीकार।

दाँव पर सब कुछ लगा है, रुक नहीं सकते।
टूट सकते हैं मगर हम झुक नहीं सकते।

We Will Not Bend

We will not bend, though we may break.
Truth does battle with Power,
Justice stands up to Tyranny;
Darkness has thrown down a challenge,
And now the last ray fades.

The flame of faith is steady in our hands,
Though lightning strikes and the earth heaves.
This is not an equal fight,
Unarmed we face the terrible enemy
Adorned with arms of every kind,
And flaunting its bestial might.

But we have vowed to take up the fight,
Angad* is on the march again,
No matter the cost, we'll keep up the fight;
We reject the call for surrender.

We cannot stop, all that we cherish is at stake.
We will not bend, though we may break.

---

*Angad, son of Bali, is portrayed as a formidably strong warrior in the Ramayana

47

हिरोशिमा की पीड़ा

किसी रात को
मेरी नींद अचानक उचट जाती है,
आँख खुल जाती है,
मैं सोचने लगता हूँ कि
जिन वैज्ञानिकों ने अणु अस्त्रों का
आविष्कार किया था:
वे हिरोशिमा-नागासाकी के
भीषण नरसंहार के समाचार सुनकर,
रात को सोये कैसे होंगे?

दाँत में फँसा तिनका,
आँख की किरकिरी,
पाँव में चुभा काँटा,
आँखों की नींद,
मन का चैन उड़ा देते हैं।

सगे-संबंधी की मृत्यु,
किसी प्रिय का न रहना,
परिचित का उठ जाना,
यहाँ तक कि पालतू पशु का भी विछोह

The Agony of Hiroshima

Sometimes at night
Suddenly, sleep deserts me,
My eyes open,
I begin to ponder—
Those scientists, who invented nuclear weapons:
On hearing of the gruesome human destruction
Of Hiroshima and Nagasaki,
How did they ever sleep at night?

A scrap caught in a tooth,
A grain of sand in the eye,
A thorn in the foot
Takes away sleep,
Peace of mind.

A death in the family,
The loss of someone we love,
The passing away of a familiar,
Even separation from a pet

हृदय में इतनी पीड़ा, इतना विषाद भर देता है कि
चेष्टा करने पर भी नींद नहीं आती है।
करवटें बदलते रात गुजर जाती है।

किंतु जिनके अविष्कार से
वह अंतिम अस्त्र बना
जिसने छ: अगस्त उन्नीस सौ पैंतालीस की काल रात्रि को
हिरोशिमा–नागासाकी में मृत्यु का ताण्डव कर
दो लाख से अधिक लोगों की बलि ले ली,
हजारों को जीवन भर के लिए अपाहिज कर दिया

क्या उन्हें एक क्षण के लिए सही, यह
अनुभूति हुई कि उनके हाथों जो कुछ
हुआ, अच्छा नहीं हुआ?
यदि हुई, तो वक्त उन्हें कटघरे में खड़ा नहीं करेगा,
किंतु यदि नहीं हुई तो इतिहास उन्हें कभी
माफ नहीं करेगा।

Breeds so much pain in the heart, such grief
That no matter how hard we try, sleep eludes us.
We toss and turn till the night is done.

But those whose invention
Created the ultimate weapon
Which, on the black night of 6 August 1945,
Unleashed the dance of death over Hiroshima
    and Nagasaki,
Causing over two hundred thousand people to
    be sacrificed,
And maiming thousands for life—

Do they, even for a moment, feel
That whatever was inflicted by them
Was monstrous?
If they do, then time will not put them in the dock,
But if they don't, then history will never
Ever forgive them.

जंग न होने देंगे

हम जंग न होने देंगे
विश्व शान्ति के हम साधक हैं, जंग न होने देंगे!

कभी न खेतों में फिर खूनी खाद फलेगी,
खलिहानों में नहीं मौत की फसल खिलेगी,
आसमान फिर कभी न अंगारे उगलेगा,
एटम से नागासाकी फिर नहीं जलेगी,
युद्धविहीन विश्व का सपना भंग न होने देंगे।
जंग न होने देंगे।

हथियारों के ढेरों पर जिनका है डेरा,
मुँह में शान्ति, बगल में बम, धोखे का फेरा,
कफन बेचने वालों से कह दो चिल्लाकर,
दुनिया जान गई है उनका असली चेहरा,
कामयाब हो उनकी चालें, ढंग न होने देंगे।
जंग न होने देंगे।

हमें चाहिए शान्ति, जिन्दगी हमको प्यारी,
हमें चाहिए शान्ति, सृजन की है तैयारी,

We Shall Not Allow War

We shall not allow war!
We are devoted to peace, we shall not allow war!

    Never again will fields bear the fruits of blood,
    Nor farms produce a harvest of death,
Never again will the sky rain fire,
Never again will Nagasaki burn,
We shall fight for our dream of a world without war.
        We shall not allow war.

Those who sit atop caches of weapons,
Mouth peace, hide bombs, spin deception,
    To those who sell shrouds—we must say,
    We have seen through your game, you will
      not succeed.
        We shall not allow war.

We want peace, life is a dear possession,
We want peace, our priority is creation—

हमने छेड़ी जंग भूख से, बीमारी से,
आगे आकर हाथ बटाए दुनिया सारी।
हरी-भरी धरती को खूनी रंग न लेने देंगे।
जंग न होने देंगे।

भारत-पाकिस्तान पड़ोसी, साथ-साथ रहना है,
प्यार करें या वार करें, दोनों को ही सहना है,
तीन बार लड़ चुके लड़ाई, कितना महँगा सौदा,
रूसी बम हो या अमेरिकी, खून एक बहना है।
जो हम पर गुजरी बच्चों के संग न होने देंगे।
जंग न होने देंगे।

Our war is against hunger and disease,
Let every man give us a helping hand.
We won't let our lush, green earth be bloodied.
                         We shall not allow war.

India and Pakistan are neighbours, we have to
    live together,
Love or battle, what we offer is what we earn,
We've fought three wars, we've paid the price,
Russian bombs or American, the blood spilt is the
    same.
We have suffered, we'll spare our children this
    fate.

                         We shall not allow war.

आओ, मन की गाँठे खोलें

यमुना तट, टीले रेतीले,
घास-फूस का घर डाँडे पर,
गोबर से लीपे आँगन में,
तुलसी का बिरवा, घण्टी स्वर,
माँ के मुँह से रामायण के दोहे-चौपाई रस घोलें!
आओ, मन की गाँठें खोलें!

बाबा की बैठक में बिछी
चटाई, बाहर रखे खड़ाऊँ,
मिलने वाले के मन में
असमंजस, जाऊँ या ना जाऊँ?
माथे तिलक, नाक पर ऐनक, पोथी खुली, स्वयं से बोलें!
आओ, मन की गाँठें खोलें!

सरस्वती की देख साधना,
लक्ष्मी ने संबंध न जोड़ा,

Come, Let Us Unravel the Knots of the Mind

The Yamuna's bank, mounds of sand,
On stilts a home of grass and thatch,
A courtyard swept with cow-dung,
Sounds of bells, the tulsi patch,
On mother's tongue the nectar of the *Ramayana's*
lines.

Come, let us unravel the knots of the mind.

In grandfather's sitting room, on the floor
A straw mat, wooden slippers outside the
door,
Those who wish to meet him, unsure:
Should they wait outside, or step indoors—
Tilak on the forehead, glasses on the nose, an open
book, he talks to himself.

Come, let us unravel the knots of the mind.

Such was his devotion to Saraswati,
He never felt the need to woo Lakshmi,

मिट्टी ने माथे का चंदन
बनने का संकल्प न छोड़ा,
नए वर्ष की अगवानी में टुक रुक लें, कुछ ताजा हो लें!
आओ, मन की गाँठें खोलें!

The earth never lost its resolve to be
Chandan* for his forehead's glory.
To welcome the new year, let us pause awhile,
refresh ourselves.

Come, let us unravel the knots of the mind.

*Auspicious sandalwood paste, applied on the forehead.

जीवन की ढलने लगी साँझ

जीवन की ढलने लगी साँझ
    उमर घट गई
    डगर कट गई
जीवन की ढलने लगी साँझ।

    बदले हैं अर्थ
    शब्द हुए व्यर्थ
शांति बिना खुशियाँ हैं बाँझ।

    सपनों से मीत
    बिखरा संगीत
ठिठक रहे पाँव और झिझक रही झाँझ।
जीवन की ढलने लगी साँझ।

The Evening of Life Begins to Fall

The evening of life begins to fall.
>My years are spent
>My journeys are done
The evening of life begins to fall.

>Meanings have changed
>Words are in vain
Without inner peace, only barren joys remain.

>Phantom friendships
>Scattered music
Faltering feet, hesitant anklets.
The evening of life begins to fall.

गीत नहीं गाता हूँ

बेनकाब चेहरे हैं,
दाग बड़े गहरे हैं,
टूटता तिलस्म, आज सच से भय खाता हूँ।
गीत नहीं गाता हूँ।

लगी कुछ ऐसी नज़र,
बिखरा शीशे सा शहर,
अपनों के मेले में मीत नहीं पाता हूँ।
गीत नहीं गाता हूँ।

पीठ में छुरी सा चाँद,
राहु गया रेखा फाँद,
मुक्ति के क्षणों में बार-बार बँध जाता हूँ।
गीत नहीं गाता हूँ।

No Longer Do I Sing

The masks have dropped away:
These scars run too deep.
The spell has broken, I face the terror of truth.
No longer do I sing.

Under the gaze of the evil eye
The city shattered like glass,
I stand friendless among my own.
No longer do I sing.

The moon is a scimitar in my back,
Rahu's fury knows no bounds;
Every moment of salvation conceals a snare.
No longer do I sing.

गीत नया गाता हूँ

टूटे हुए तारों से फूटे वासन्ती स्वर,
पत्थर की छाती में उग आया नव अंकुर,
 झरे सब पीले पात,
 कोयल की कुहुक रात,
प्राची में अरुणिमा की रेख देख पाता हूँ।
 गीत नया गाता हूँ।

टूटे हुए सपने की सुने कौन सिसकी?
अन्तर को चीर व्यथा पलकों पर ठिठकी।
 हार नहीं मानूँगा,
 रार नई ठानूँगा,
काल के कपाल पर लिखता-मिटाता हूँ।
 गीत नया गाता हूँ।

I Sing A New Song

From broken strings erupt the notes of spring,
A new seed sprouts in the heart of stone,
    All the yellowed leaves have fallen,
    The night resounds to the *koel's* call,
In the east I see the faint glow of dawn.
    I sing a new song.

Who wants to hear a broken dream's sighs?
Pain tears through the heart, and halts at the eyes.
    I will not give in,
    I will wage a new fight,
On time's brow I write and erase as I go along.
    I sing a new song.

Notes

1. 'A New Milestone' was written on his sixty-first birthday.
2. 'Anguish' is from the diary he kept while in jail during the Emergency (1975–77).
3. 'A Year Has Gone By' was written during the Emergency, on the completion of a year in jail.
4. 'Never Place Me So High' was written after a felicitation function held in Delhi on 24 April 1992 on being conferred the Padma Vibhushan, India's second highest civilian decoration.
5. 'Who Are the Kauravas, and Who the Pandavas' draws upon episodes in the epic *Mahabharata*. The Kauravas and Pandavas were cousins who fought each other in the battle of Kurukshetra. The Pandavas were aided by Lord Krishna—though he did not take up weapons on their behalf, he showed them the path of dharma, or righteousness and duty. The war had its beginnings in a game of dice, which the Kauravas won because of the unfair means they were encouraged to adopt by their maternal uncle, Shakuni. Yuddhishtir (also known as Dharmaraj, or the king of dharma), the oldest of the Pandava brothers, lost all his possessions, his kingdom, and finally even Draupadi, wife of the Pandavas. Draupadi was publicly humiliated by the Kauravas in court.
6. 'A Battle with Death' resulted from emotions written down one night in New York when he was seriously ill.
7. 'We Will Not Bend' was written in 1975, while in jail during the Emergency.
8. 'Come, Let Us Unravel the Knots of the Mind', written on his birthday in 1994, recalls an idyllic childhood.
9. 'The Evening of Life Begins to Fall' was written during the Emergency on his fiftieth birthday.